To: My Lenora
With Love Always

From:

Mom

MERRY CHRISTMAS

easy meals

chicken

BARNES
&NOBLE
BOOKS
NEW YORK

This edition published by Barnes & Noble Inc.,
by arrangement with Parragon

2002 Barnes & Noble Books

M 1 0 9 8 7 6 5 4 3 2 1

ISBN: 0-7607-3297-3

Printed in Spain

Produced by The Bridgewater Book Company Ltd, Lewes, East Sussex, United Kingdom

Acknowledgements
Creative Director Terry Jeavons
Art Director Sarah Howerd
Editorial Director Fiona Biggs
Senior Editor Mark Truman
Editorial Assistants Simon Bailey, Tom Kitch
Page Make-up Chris Akroyd

NOTES FOR THE READER

- This book uses both US and metric measurements. Follow the same units of measurement throughout; do not mix US and metric.
- All spoon measurements are level: teaspoons are assumed to be 5 ml, and tablespoons are assumed to be 15 ml.
- Cup measurements in this book are for American cups.
- Unless otherwise stated, milk is assumed to be whole milk, eggs and individual vegetables such as potatoes are medium-sized, and pepper is freshly ground black pepper.
- Recipes using raw or very lightly cooked eggs should be avoided by infants, the elderly, pregnant women, convalescents, and anyone suffering from an illness.
- Optional ingredients, variations or serving suggestions have not been included in the calculations.
- The times given are an approximate guide only. Preparation times differ according to the techniques used by different people, and the cooking times vary as a result of the type of oven used.

Contents

Introduction

When it comes to planning meals that are quick and easy to prepare and cook, chicken can be a star ingredient. A chicken portion may be prepared very simply in numerous ways: brushed with olive oil and broiled, and served with rice and a fresh green salad, or roasted in the oven with herbs and served with potatoes and vegetables. A chicken half makes the ultimate easy meal. It may be cut into strips and and added to a stir-fry, or added to pasta or risotto. Chicken Risotto à la Milanese is made with saffron, producing a lovely golden color.

If you want to prepare your meal and pop it in the oven while you have a long soak in the bath after a busy day, use chicken as a base for a hearty soup, such as Wild Rice & Smoked Chicken Chowder, or for a casserole such as Chicken Basquaise, in which chicken and rice are cooked together in one pot.

guide to recipe key	
easy	Recipes are graded as follows: 1 pea—easy; 2 peas—very easy; 3 peas—extremely easy.
serves 4	Most of the recipes in this book serve four people. Simply halve the ingredients to serve two, taking care not to mix US and metric measurements.
15 minutes	Preparation time. Where recipes include marinating, soaking, standing, or chilling, times for these are listed separately: eg, 15 minutes, plus 1 hour to marinate.
15 minutes	Cooking time. Cooking times do not include the cooking of rice served with the main dishes.

For an informal meal for guests, recipes like Murgh Pullau or Jambalaya are fun, and for an elegant dinner try Squabs with Fruity Rice Stuffing. This dish traditionally uses game hens from Cornwall in southwest England, stuffed with rice and chestnuts, raisins, and apricots, and flavored with port.

Chicken is inexpensive, low in fat, and easy to digest, so it fits perfectly into a busy modern life. The following pages give ideas for using chicken in snacks and salads, as well as in soups and main-course meals, exploring its natural versatility.

Braised Chicken with Garlic & Spices, page 82

Soups

Chicken soup is best known as a comforting food, and indeed, thick soups such as Chicken, Corn & Bean are perfect for warming you up after a walk on a cold winter's day. Yet chicken soup can also be light and nutritious—Chicken and Spring Vegetable Soup will sharpen the appetite of a convalescent, and restore strength. Chicken soups can also be delicious and elegant. For a soup to begin a Thai meal, Chicken, Leek & Celery is flavored with coconut milk and nutmeg. Chicken, Avocado & Chipotle Soup combines chicken with spicy Mexican flavors.

Chicken & Rice Soup

6¼ cups chicken
    bouillon
2 small carrots, sliced
    very thinly
1 celery stalk, diced finely
1 baby leek, sliced thinly
4 oz/115 g fresh baby
    peas, or defrosted
    frozen baby peas
1 cup cooked rice
5½ oz/150 g cooked
    chicken meat, sliced
2 tsp chopped fresh
    tarragon
1 tbsp chopped fresh
    parsley
salt and pepper
parsley sprigs,
    to garnish

 extremely easy

serves 4

15 minutes

35–40 minutes

❶ Pour the bouillon into a large pan and add the carrots, celery, and leek. Bring to a boil, then reduce the heat to low and simmer gently, partially covered, for 10 minutes.

❷ Stir in the peas, rice, and chicken meat, and continue cooking for 10–15 minutes more, or until the chicken is cooked through and the vegetables are tender.

❸ Add the chopped tarragon and parsley, then taste and adjust the seasoning, adding salt and pepper as needed.

❹ Ladle the soup into warm soup bowls and garnish with sprigs of parsley, then serve.

COOK'S TIP
If the bouillon you are using is a little weak, or made with a bouillon cube, add the herbs at the beginning, so they can flavor the bouillon for longer.

Chicken, Corn & Bean Soup

INGREDIENTS

1½ tbsp butter
1 large onion, chopped
    finely
1 garlic clove, chopped
    finely
3 tbsp all-purpose flour
2½ cups water
4 cups chicken bouillon
1 carrot, sliced thinly
6 oz/175 g green beans,
    trimmed and cut into
    short pieces
14 oz/400 g canned wax
    beans, drained and
    rinsed
12 oz/350 g cooked corn
    or frozen corn kernels
8 oz/225 g cooked
    chicken meat
salt and pepper

 extremely easy

 serves 4

10 minutes

1 hour

❶ Melt the butter in a large pan over a medium–low heat. Add the onion and garlic, and cook, stirring frequently, for 3–4 minutes, or until just softened.

❷ Stir in the flour and continue cooking for 2 minutes, stirring occasionally.

❸ Stir in the water little by little, scraping the bottom of the pan to mix in the flour. Bring to a boil, stirring, and cook for 2 minutes. Add the bouillon and stir until smooth.

❹ Add the carrot, green beans, wax beans, corn, and the chicken meat. Season with salt and pepper. Cover the pan, return to a boil, reduce the heat to medium–low, and simmer for about 35 minutes, or until the vegetables are tender.

❺ Taste the soup and adjust the seasoning, adding salt, if needed, and plenty of pepper.

❻ Ladle the soup into warm, deep bowls, and serve hot.

VARIATION

Replace the wax beans with 10½ oz/ 300 g cooked fresh fava beans, peeled, or lima beans. You could also substitute sliced runner beans for the green beans.

Chicken, Leek & Celery Soup

4 cups chicken bouillon
1 bay leaf
7 oz/200 g skinless boned chicken halves
4 tbsp all-purpose flour
2 tsp butter
1 small onion, chopped finely
3 large leeks, including green parts, sliced thinly
2 celery stalks, peeled and sliced thinly
2 tbsp heavy cream
freshly grated nutmeg
salt and pepper
fresh cilantro or parsley, to garnish

❶ Heat the bouillon in a pan with the bay leaf until the bouillon is steaming. Add the chicken halves and simmer for 20 minutes, or until firm to the touch. Discard the bay leaf and remove the chicken. When it is cool, cut into small cubes.

❷ Put the flour in a bowl. Very slowly whisk in enough bouillon to make a smooth liquid, adding about half the bouillon.

❸ Heat the butter in a pan, then add the onion, leeks, and half of the celery. Cook for 5 minutes, stirring frequently, until the leeks begin to soften. Pour in the flour and bouillon mixture slowly, and bring to a boil, stirring constantly. Stir in the remaining bouillon. Reduce the heat, cover, and simmer for about 25 minutes, or until the vegetables are tender.

❹ Let the soup cool slightly, then transfer to a blender or a food processor and purée until smooth; work in batches, if necessary. (If using a food processor, strain off the liquid and reserve. Purée the soup solids with enough liquid to moisten them, then combine with the remaining liquid.)

❺ Return the soup to the pan and stir in the cream and nutmeg. Season to taste. Place over a low heat. Add the chicken and remaining celery, then simmer for 15 minutes, or until the celery is tender. Serve, sprinkled with cilantro.

easy

serves 4

15 minutes, plus 30 minutes to cool

1 hour, 10 minutes

Chicken & Spring Vegetable Soup

INGREDIENTS

4 cups chicken bouillon
6 oz/175 g skinless
*   boned chicken halves*
fresh parsley and
*   tarragon sprigs*
2 garlic cloves, crushed
4½ oz/125 g baby
*   carrots, halved or cut*
*   into fourths*
8 oz/225 g small new
*   potatoes, cut into*
*   fourths*
4 tbsp all-purpose flour
½ cup milk
4–5 scallions, sliced at
*   a diagonal angle*
3 oz/85 g asparagus
*   tips, halved and cut*
*   into 1½ inch/4 cm*
*   pieces*
½ cup heavy cream
1 tbsp finely chopped
*   fresh parsley*
1 tbsp finely chopped
*   fresh tarragon*
salt and pepper

❶ Put the bouillon in a pan with the chicken, parsley and tarragon sprigs, and garlic. Bring just to a boil, then reduce the heat and simmer, covered, for 20 minutes, or until the chicken is cooked through and firm to the touch.

❷ Remove the chicken and strain the bouillon. When the chicken is cool enough to handle, cut into bite-size pieces.

❸ Return the bouillon to the pan and bring to a boil. Adjust the heat so the liquid boils very gently. Add the carrots, then cover and cook for 5 minutes. Put in the potatoes and cover again, then cook for about 12 minutes, or until the vegetables are beginning to become tender.

❹Meanwhile, put the flour in a small mixing bowl and very slowly whisk in the milk to make a thick paste. Stir in a little of the hot bouillon mixture to make a smooth liquid.

❺ Stir in the flour mixture and bring just to a boil, stirring. Boil gently for 4–5 minutes until it thickens, stirring frequently.

❻ Add the scallions, asparagus, and chicken. Reduce the heat a little and simmer for about 15 minutes, or until all the vegetables are tender. Stir in the cream and herbs. Season and serve.

 easy

serves 4

15 minutes

1¼ hours

Chicken & Chickpea Soup with Fruit

1 lb 12 oz/800 g chicken legs or thighs, skinned
1 celery stalk, sliced
1 large carrot, halved and sliced
1 large onion, chopped finely
2 garlic cloves, chopped finely
10 cups chicken bouillon
4–5 parsley stems
1 bay leaf
4½ oz/125 g lean smoked ham, diced
14 oz/400 g canned chickpeas, rinsed
1 large turnip, diced
2 zucchini, halved and sliced
1 large potato, diced
1 sweet potato, diced
6 oz/175 g corn kernels
3 large pears, peeled, cored, and cubed
3 tbsp fresh lime juice
2 tbsp olive oil
2 very unripe bananas, cut into ¼ inch/5 mm slices
salt and pepper
chopped fresh parsley, to garnish

easy

serves 4

35 minutes

1 hour, 35 minutes

❶ Put the chicken into a large 2 quart/2.5 liter pan with the celery, carrot, onion, garlic, bouillon, parsley stems, and bay leaf. Bring just to a boil over a medium–high heat and skim off any foam that rises to the surface. Reduce the heat and simmer, partially covered, for about 45 minutes, or until the chicken is tender.

❷ Remove the chicken from the bouillon. When it is cool, remove the meat from the bones, then cut into cubes and reserve. Skim the fat from the bouillon. Discard the parsley stems and the bay leaf.

❸ Bring the bouillon just to a boil. Add the ham, chickpeas, turnip, zucchini, potato, sweet potato, and corn. Return the meat to the bouillon. Adjust the heat so the soup simmers gently and cook, partially covered, for about 30 minutes, or until all the vegetables are tender.

❹ Add the pears and lime juice to the soup, and continue cooking for 5 minutes, or until they are barely poached. Season to taste, adding more lime juice to taste.

❺ Heat the oil in a skillet over a medium–high heat. Fry the bananas until they are golden. Drain on paper towels and keep warm. Ladle the soup into bowls, and top with fried banana slices, then garnish with parsley.

Chicken, Avocado & Chipotle Soup

INGREDIENTS

6¼ cups chicken
  bouillon
2–3 garlic cloves,
  chopped finely
1–2 chipotle chilis, cut
  into very thin strips
  (see Cook's Tip)
1 avocado
lime or lemon juice,
  for tossing
3–5 scallions, sliced
  thinly
12–14 oz/350–400 g
  cooked chicken
  breast meat, torn or
  cut into shreds
2 tbsp chopped fresh
  cilantro
1 lime, cut into wedges,
  to serve

extremely easy

serves 4

15 minutes

10–15 minutes

❶ Put the garlic and the chipotle chilis into a pan, pour the bouillon over them, and bring to a boil.

❷ Meanwhile, cut the avocado in half around the pit. Twist the two halves apart, then remove the pit with a knife. Peel off the skin carefully, and dice the flesh, then toss in lime or lemon juice to prevent discoloration.

❸ Arrange the scallions, chicken, avocado, and fresh cilantro in the base of 4 soup bowls or in a large serving bowl, and sprinkle the coriander over the top.

❹ Ladle the hot bouillon over and serve each bowl with lime wedges and perhaps a handful of tortilla chips.

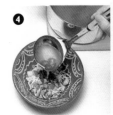

COOK'S TIP
This dish makes an elegant appetizer served layered with rounds of crisp tortillas, like a stacked tostada.

Cream of Lemon & Chicken with Spaghetti

INGREDIENTS

4 tbsp butter
8 shallots, sliced thinly
2 carrots, sliced thinly
2 celery stalks, sliced
    thinly
8 oz/225 g boned
    chicken breasts,
    chopped finely
3 lemons
5 cups chicken bouillon
8 oz/225 g dried
    spaghetti, broken
    into small pieces
⅔ cup heavy cream
salt and white pepper

GARNISH
fresh parsley sprig
3 lemon slices, halved

 very easy

 serves 4

 15 minutes

 1¼ hours

COOK'S TIP
You can prepare this soup up to the end of step 3 in advance. Heat the soup through before serving, add the pasta, and complete step 4 and step 5.

❶ Melt the butter in a large pan. Add the shallots, carrots, celery, and chicken and panfry over a low heat, stirring occasionally, for 8 minutes.

❷ Thinly pare the lemons and blanch the lemon zest in boiling water for 3 minutes. Squeeze the juice from the lemons.

❸ Add the lemon zest and juice to the pan with the chicken bouillon. Bring to a boil slowly over a low heat, and simmer for 40 minutes.

❹ Add the spaghetti to the pan, breaking it into small pieces as you do so, and cook for 15 minutes. Season to taste with salt and white pepper, and add the cream. Heat through, but do not let the soup boil or it will curdle.

❺ Pour the soup into a tureen or 4 individual bowls, and garnish the tureen or each bowl with the parsley and half slices of lemon, and serve the soup immediately.

Cream of Chicken & Tomato Soup

INGREDIENTS

4 tbsp unsalted butter
1 large onion, chopped
1 lb 2 oz/500 g chicken,
  shredded very finely
2½ cups chicken
  bouillon
6 medium tomatoes,
  chopped finely
pinch of baking soda
1 tbsp superfine sugar
⅔ cup heavy cream
salt and pepper
fresh basil leaves,
  to garnish
croûtons, to serve

❶ Melt the butter in a large pan, and panfry the onion and shredded chicken for 5 minutes.

❷ Add 1¼ cups chicken bouillon to the pan, with the tomatoes and baking soda.

❸ Bring the soup to a boil and simmer for 20 minutes.

❹ Let the soup cool, then blend in a food processor.

❺ Return the soup to the pan and add the remaining chicken bouillon, then season and add the sugar. Pour the soup into a tureen and add a swirl of heavy cream. Serve the soup with croûtons and garnish with basil.

very easy

serves 4

15 minutes

40 minutes

COOK'S TIP
For a healthier version of this soup, use light cream and omit the sugar.

light Meals & Salads

Chicken is an international food, so these pages contain plenty of ideas for turning even a light lunch or supper dish into something special. If you love Mexican food, try Chicken Tostadas — layered beans, cheese, chicken, and salad served on a crisp corn tortilla and topped with dried chilis. Indonesian Potato & Chicken Salad is an unusual combination of chicken with vegetables, pineapple, and peanuts in a spicy peanut butter dressing. The chapter ends in Italy with a Chicken Risotto à la Milanese.

Chicken & Mushroom Soup with a Puff Pastry Top

INGREDIENTS

5½ cups bouillon
4 skinless boned
   chicken halves
2 garlic cloves, crushed
small bunch of fresh
   tarragon, or
   ¼ tsp dried tarragon
1 tbsp butter
14 oz/400 g chestnut or
   porcini mushrooms,
   sliced
3 tbsp dry white wine
6 tbsp all-purpose flour
¾ cup heavy cream
13½ oz/390 g puff
   pastry
2 tbsp chopped finely
   fresh parsley
salt and pepper

❶ Pour the bouillon into a pan and bring it to a boil. Add the chicken, garlic, and tarragon, reduce the heat, cover, and simmer for 20 minutes, or until cooked. Remove the chicken and when it is cool, cut it into cubes. Strain the bouillon.

❷ Melt the butter in a skillet over a medium heat, then add the mushrooms and seasoning. Panfry for 5–8 minutes, or until golden brown, stirring as the mushrooms color. Add the wine and bubble briefly, then remove from the heat.

❸ Put the flour in a bowl and whisk in the cream to make a thick paste. Stir in some bouillon to make a smooth liquid. Bring the remaining bouillon to a boil in a pan. Whisk in the flour mixture, then boil gently for 3–4 minutes, or until the soup thickens, stirring often. Add the mushrooms and liquid, if any. Reduce the heat and simmer gently, just to keep warm.

❹ Cut out 6 pastry circles smaller than the soup bowls. Put on a cookie sheet, prick with a fork, and bake in a preheated oven at 400° F/200° C for 15 minutes, or until golden.

❺ Meanwhile, add the chicken to the soup, season, simmer for about 10 minutes, and stir in the parsley. Ladle the soup into bowls, place the pastry circles on top, and serve.

 easy

 serves 4

 15 minutes

50 minutes

Wild Rice & Smoked Chicken Chowder

INGREDIENTS

½ cup wild rice, washed
3 fresh corn cob ears,
    husks and silks
    removed
2 tbsp vegetable oil
1 large onion, chopped
    finely
1 celery stalk, sliced
    thinly
1 leek, trimmed and
    sliced thinly
½ tsp dried thyme
2 tbsp all-purpose flour
14 cups chicken bouillon
9 oz/250 g boned
    smoked chicken,
    skinned, diced, or
    shredded
1 cup heavy or
    whipping cream
1 tbsp chopped fresh dill
salt and pepper
fresh dill sprigs,
    to garnish

❶ Bring a large pan of water to a boil. Add 1 tablespoon of salt and sprinkle in the wild rice. Return to a boil, then cover the pan, reduce the heat, and simmer for about 40 minutes, or until tender but still firm to the bite. Do not overcook the rice, because it will continue to cook in the soup. Drain and rinse the rice, then set it aside.

❷ Hold the corn cobs vertical to a cutting board and, using a sharp heavy knife, cut down along the cobs to remove the kernels. Set them aside. Scrape the cob to remove the milky juices, and reserve them for the soup.

❸ Heat the oil in a large pan, then add the onion, celery, leek, and dried thyme. Cook, stirring frequently, for about 8 minutes, or until the vegetables are very soft.

❹ Sprinkle the flour over the vegetables and stir until it is blended in. Whisk in the bouillon, a little at a time, add the corn with any juices, and bring to a boil, skimming off any foam. Reduce the heat and simmer for 25 minutes, or until the vegetables are soft and tender.

❺ Stir in the smoked chicken, wild rice, cream, and dill, and season with salt and pepper. Simmer for 10 minutes, or until heated through. Garnish with dill sprigs and serve at once.

 very easy

 serves 4

 15 minutes

 1 hour

Chicken & Sausage Gumbo

INGREDIENTS

2 lb 12 oz/1.25 kg chicken
¾ cup all-purpose flour
¾ cup vegetable oil
1 lb 9 oz/700 g andouille or other smoked pork sausage, cut into 2 inch/5 cm pieces
2 large onions, chopped
3–4 celery stalks, chopped finely
2 green bell peppers, cored, seeded, and chopped finely
1 lb 9 oz/700 g okra, trimmed and cut into ½ inch/1 cm pieces
4 garlic cloves, chopped
2 bay leaves
½ tsp cayenne pepper
1 tsp black pepper
1 tsp mustard powder
1 tsp dried thyme
½ tsp ground cumin
½ tsp dried oregano
6¼ cups chicken bouillon, simmering
3–4 ripe tomatoes, seeded and chopped
salt
2 cups cooked long-grain white rice, to serve

❶ Cut the chicken into 8 pieces and toss it in 2 tablespoons of flour. Heat 2 tablespoons of the oil in a skillet. Add the chicken and panfry for 10 minutes, or until golden. Set aside.

❷ Add the sausage pieces to the pan, stirring and tossing, for about 5 minutes, or until they begin to color. Set aside.

❸ Heat the remaining oil in the cleaned pan until it begins to smoke. Add all the remaining flour at once and whisk it into the oil. Reduce the heat and cook, stirring frequently, for 20 minutes, or until the roux is a deep rich brown.

❹ Add the onions, celery, and bell peppers to the roux, and fry, stirring frequently, until they begin to soften. Stir in the okra, garlic, bay leaves, cayenne pepper, black pepper, mustard powder, thyme, cumin, and oregano, and stir well.

❺ Whisk the hot bouillon into the mixture a little at a time, stirring well after each addition. Simmer for 10 minutes. Stir in the reserved sausage, tomatoes, and the chicken pieces, and simmer for 20 minutes, or until tender.

❻ To serve, fill a cup with rice, packing it lightly, then unmold it into the center of a wide soup bowl. Spoon the gumbo around the rice, and serve immediately.

 very easy

 serves 4

 20 minutes

 1 hour, 20 minutes

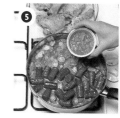

Pad Thai

INGREDIENTS

8 oz/225 g flat rice noodles (sen lek)
2 tbsp peanut or vegetable oil
8 oz/225 g boneless chicken halves, skinned and sliced
4 shallots, chopped finely
2 garlic cloves, chopped
4 scallions, cut at a diagonal angle into 2 inch/5 cm pieces
12 oz/350 g fresh white crab meat
1 cup fresh bean sprouts, rinsed
1 tbsp preserved radish or fresh radish, diced
2–4 tbsp roasted peanuts, chopped
fresh cilantro sprigs, to garnish

SAUCE
3 tbsp Thai fish sauce
2–3 tbsp rice vinegar
1 tbsp chili bean sauce
1 tbsp toasted sesame oil
1 tbsp palm sugar
½ tsp cayenne pepper

❶ To make the sauce, whisk together the sauce ingredients in a small bowl, and set aside.

❷ Put the rice noodles in a large bowl and pour enough hot water over to cover them. Let stand for 15 minutes, or until softened. Drain, rinse, and drain again, and set aside.

❸ Heat the oil in a heavy-based wok over high heat until very hot, but not smoking. Add the chicken strips and stir-fry for 1–2 minutes, or until they just begin to color. Using a slotted spoon, transfer to a plate. Reduce the heat to medium–high.

❹ Stir the shallots, garlic, and scallions into the wok, and stir-fry for about 1 minute. Stir in the drained noodles, then the prepared sauce.

❺ Return the reserved chicken to the pan with the crab meat, bean sprouts, and radish. Toss well, then cook for about 5 minutes, or until heated, tossing frequently. If the noodles begin to stick, add a little water to the pan.

❻ Turn into a serving dish and sprinkle with the chopped peanuts. Garnish with cilantro and serve immediately.

extremely easy

serves 4

15 minutes, plus 15 minutes to stand

10 minutes

Pozole

INGREDIENTS

1 lb/450 g pork for
  stewing, such as
  lean belly
½ small chicken
about 8 cups water
1 chicken bouillon cube
1 whole garlic bulb,
  divided into cloves
  but not peeled
1 onion, chopped
2 bay leaves
1 lb/450 g cooked
  hominy
¼–½ tsp ground cumin
salt and pepper

TO SERVE
½ small to medium
  cabbage, sliced thinly
dried oregano leaves
dried chili flakes
tortilla chips
lime wedges

❶ Place the pork and chicken in a large pan. Add enough water to fill the pan. (Do not worry about having too much bouillon—it keeps fresh up to a week, and freezes well.)

❷ Bring to a boil, then skim off the fat that rises to the surface. Reduce the heat and add the bouillon cube, garlic, onion, and bay leaves. Simmer, covered, over a medium–low heat until the pork and chicken are tender and cooked through.

❸ Remove the pork and chicken from the soup and let cool. When cool enough to handle, remove the chicken flesh from the bones and cut the pork into cubes. Set aside.

❹ Skim the fat off the soup and discard the bay leaves. Add the hominy and cumin, and season with salt and pepper to taste. Bring to a boil.

❺ To serve, place a little pork and chicken in soup bowls. Top with cabbage, oregano, and chili flakes, then spoon them into the hot soup. Serve piping hot, with lime wedges for squeezing and perhaps a handful of tortilla chips.

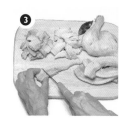

 very easy

 serves 4

 15 minutes

40 minutes

Chicken Tacos from Puebla

INGREDIENTS

8 soft corn tortillas
2 tsp vegetable oil
8–12 oz / 225–350 g left-
over cooked chicken,
diced or shredded
8 oz / 225 g canned
refried beans,
warmed, and thinned
with 2 tbsp water
¼ tsp ground cumin
¼ tsp dried oregano
1 avocado, pitted, sliced,
and tossed with lime
juice
salsa verde, or salsa of
your choice
1 canned chipotle chili in
adobo marinade,
chopped, or bottled
chipotle salsa
¾ cup sour cream
½ onion, chopped
handful of lettuce leaves
5 radishes, diced
salt and pepper

❶ Warm a an ungreased, nonstick skillet over a medium heat, and stack the tortillas in it to heat. Alternate the top and bottom tortillas so that the stack heats evenly. Wrap in aluminum foil, or a clean dish towel, to keep warm.

❷ Heat the oil in a skillet, add the chicken, and heat through. Season with salt and pepper to taste.

❸ Combine the refried beans with the cumin and oregano.

❹ Spread one tortilla with warm refried beans, then top with a spoonful of chicken, a slice or two of avocado, a dab of salsa, chipotle to taste, a spoonful of sour cream, and a sprinkling of onion, lettuce, and radishes. Season with salt and pepper to taste, then roll up. Repeat with the remaining tortillas, and serve the tacos at once.

 extremely easy

 serves 4

 20 minutes

 20 minutes

Chicken Tostadas with Green Salsa & Chipotle

INGREDIENTS

vegetable oil, for frying
6 soft corn tortillas
1 lb/450 g chicken meat,
    cut into strips,
    or diced
1 cup chicken bouillon
2 garlic cloves,
    chopped finely
14 oz/400 g refried
    beans, fresh or dried
large pinch ground cumin
8 oz/225 g grated cheese
1 tbsp chopped fresh
    cilantro
2 ripe tomatoes, diced
handful of crisp lettuce
    leaves, such as
    Romaine or iceberg,
    shredded
4–6 radishes, diced
3 scallions, sliced thinly
1 ripe avocado, pitted,
    diced or sliced, and
    tossed with lime juice
soured cream to taste
1–2 canned chipotle
    chilis in adobo
    marinade, or dried
    chipotle reconstituted,
    cut into thin strips

❶ To make tostadas, panfry the tortillas in a small amount of oil in a nonstick skillet until crisp.

❷ Put the chicken in a pan with the bouillon and garlic. Bring to a boil, then reduce the heat and panfry for 1–2 minutes, or until the chicken begins to turn opaque.

❸ Remove the chicken from the heat and let it steep in the hot liquid to cook through.

❹ Heat the beans with enough water to form a smooth purée. Add the cumin and keep warm.

❺ Reheat the tostadas under a preheated broiler, if necessary. Spread the hot beans on the tostadas, then sprinkle with the grated cheese. Lift the cooked chicken from the liquid and divide between the tostadas. Sprinkle with the cilantro and top with the tomatoes, lettuce, radishes, scallions, avocado, sour cream, and a few strips of chipotle. Serve immediately.

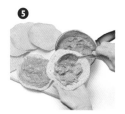

 extremely easy

 serves 4

 20 minutes

 20 minutes

Green Chile & Chicken Chilaquiles

INGREDIENTS

12 stale tortillas, cut
    into strips
1 tbsp vegetable oil
1 small cooked chicken,
    meat removed from
    the bones and cut
    into bite-size pieces
salsa verde
8 tbsp chopped fresh
    cilantro
1 tsp finely chopped
    fresh oregano
    or thyme
4 garlic cloves, chopped
    finely
¼ tsp ground cumin
2 cups chicken bouillon
12 oz/350 g grated
    cheese, such as
    Cheddar, Manchego,
    or mozzarella
about 1⅓ cups freshly
    grated Parmesan
    cheese

TO SERVE
1½ cups crème fraîche or
    sour cream
3–5 scallions, sliced
    thinly
pickled chilis

❶ Place the tortilla strips in a roasting pan, toss with the oil, then bake in a preheated oven at 375°F/190°C for about 30 minutes, or until they are crisp and golden.

❷ Arrange the chicken in a 9 x 13 inch/22.5 x 32.5 cm casserole, then sprinkle with half the salsa verde, and with the cilantro, oregano, garlic, cumin, and cheese. Repeat these layers and top with the tortilla strips.

❸ Pour the bouillon over the top, then sprinkle with the remaining cheeses.

❹ Bake in a preheated oven at 375°F/190°C for about 30 minutes, or until the cheese is lightly golden in areas.

❺ Garnish with the crème fraîche, scallions, and pickled chilis to taste. Serve at once.

 extremely easy

 serves 4

 15 minutes

 1 hour

Lemon Grass Chicken Skewers

INGREDIENTS

2 long or 4 short lemon
  grass stalks
2 large boneless,
  skinless chicken
  breasts, about
  14 oz/400 g in total
1 small egg white
1 carrot, grated finely
1 small red chile, seeded
  and chopped
2 tbsp chopped fresh
  garlic chives
2 tbsp chopped fresh
  cilantro
1 tbsp sunflower oil
salt and pepper
cilantro and lime slices,
  to garnish

 very easy

 serves 4

 15 minutes,
  plus 15 minutes
  to chill

 4–6 minutes

COOK'S TIP

If whole lemon grass
stalks are not available,
use wooden or bamboo
skewers and add
$\frac{1}{2}$ teaspoon of ground
lemon grass to the
mixture with the other
flavorings.

❶ If the lemon grass stalks are long, cut them in half across the middle to make 4 short lengths. Cut each stalk in half lengthwise, so you have 8 sticks.

❷ Chop the chicken pieces roughly, and place them in a food processor with the egg white. Process to a smooth paste, then add the carrot, chile, chives, cilantro, and salt and pepper. Process for a few seconds to mix well.

❸ Chill the mixture in the refrigerator for about 15 minutes. Divide the mixture into 8 equal portions, and use your hands to shape the mixture around the skewers fashioned from lemon grass.

❹ Brush the skewers and broil them under a preheated medium–hot broiler for 4–6 minutes, turning them occasionally, until they are golden brown and cooked thoroughly. Alternatively, grill over medium–hot coals.

❺ Serve hot, with cilantro and lime slices to garnish.

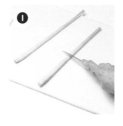

Chicken Balls with Dipping Sauce

INGREDIENTS

2 large boneless,
  skinless chicken
  halves
3 tbsp vegetable oil
2 shallots, chopped
  finely
½ celery stalk, chopped
  finely
1 garlic clove, crushed
2 tbsp light soy sauce
1 small egg
1 bunch scallions
salt and pepper
scallion tassels,
  to garnish

DIPPING SAUCE
3 tbsp dark soy sauce
1 tbsp rice wine
1 tsp sesame seeds

❶ Cut the chicken into ¾ inch/2 cm pieces. Heat half of the oil in a wok, and stir-fry the chicken quickly over a high heat for 2–3 minutes, or until golden. Remove the chicken from the wok with a perforated spoon, and set aside.

❷ Add the shallots, celery, and garlic to the wok, and stir-fry for 1–2 minutes, or until softened but not browned.

❸ Place the chicken, shallots, celery, and garlic in a food processor, and process until ground finely. Add 1 tablespoon of light soy, salt and pepper, and just enough egg to make a fairly firm mixture.

❹ Trim the scallions and cut into 2 inch/5 cm lengths. Make the dipping sauce by mixing together the dark soy sauce, rice wine, and sesame seeds, then set aside.

❺ Shape the chicken mixture into 16–18 walnut-sized balls. Heat the remaining oil in a wok, and stir-fry the chicken balls in small batches for 4–5 minutes, or until golden brown. Drain on paper towels and keep hot.

❻ Stir-fry the scallions for 1–2 minutes to soften, then stir in the remaining light soy sauce. Serve with the chicken balls and the dipping sauce. Serve on a plate, garnished with scallions cut into tassels.

 easy

 serves 4

15 minutes

about 30 minutes

Rice Noodles with Chicken & Bok Choy

INGREDIENTS

7 oz/200 g rice stick
    noodles
1 tbsp sunflower oil
1 garlic clove, chopped
    finely
¾ inch/2 cm piece fresh
    ginger, chopped
    finely
4 scallions, chopped
1 bird's eye red chile,
    seeded and sliced
10½ oz/300 g boneless,
    skinless chicken,
    chopped finely
2 chicken livers,
    chopped finely
1 celery stalk, sliced
    thinly
1 carrot, cut into fine
    short, thin sticks
5½ cups shredded bok
    choy
4 tbsp lime juice
2 tbsp Thai fish sauce
1 tbsp soy sauce

TO GARNISH
2 tbsp fresh chopped
    mint
slices of pickled garlic

❶ Soak the rice noodles in hot water for 15 minutes, or according to the package directions. Drain well.

❷ Heat the oil in a wok and stir-fry the garlic, ginger, scallions, and chile for about 1 minute. Stir in the chicken and chicken livers, then stir-fry over a high heat for 2–3 minutes, or until they just begin to brown.

❸ Stir in the celery and carrot, and stir-fry for another 2 minutes to soften them. Add the bok choy, then stir in the lime juice, fish sauce, and soy sauce.

❹ Add the noodles and stir to heat thoroughly. Sprinkle with mint and pickled garlic. Serve immediately.

 extremely easy

 serves 4

 15 minutes,
    plus 15 minutes
    to soak

 10 minutes

Indonesian Potato & Chicken Salad

INGREDIENTS

4 large waxy potatoes,
  diced
300 g/10½ oz fresh
  pineapple, diced, or
  canned, unsweetened
  pineapple chunks
2 carrots, grated
6 oz/175 g beansprouts
1 bunch scallions, sliced
1 large zucchini, cut into
  short, thin sticks
3 celery stalks, cut into
  short, thin sticks
6 oz/175 g unsalted
  peanuts
2 cooked chicken fillets,
  about 4½ oz/
  125 g each, sliced
lime wedges, to garnish

DRESSING
6 tbsp crunchy peanut
  butter
6 tbsp olive oil
2 tbsp light soy sauce
1 red chile, chopped
2 tsp sesame oil
4 tsp lime juice

❶ Cook the diced potatoes in a pan of boiling water for 10 minutes, or until tender. Drain and let cool.

❷ Transfer the cooled potatoes to a salad bowl.

❸ Add the diced fresh pineapple, to the potatoes. If using canned pineapple chunks, drain them, and rinse in cold running water before adding. Add the carrots, beansprouts, scallions, zucchini, celery, peanuts, and sliced chicken. Toss well to mix all the salad ingredients together.

❹ To make the dressing, put the peanut butter in a bowl. Whisk in the olive oil and light soy sauce a little at a time.

❺ Stir in the chopped red chile, sesame oil, and lime juice. Mix until well combined.

❻ Pour the spicy dressing over the salad and toss lightly to coat all of the ingredients. Serve the salad immediately, garnished with the lime wedges.

 extremely easy

 serves 4

20 minutes

10 minutes

Potato, Chicken & Banana Cake

INGREDIENTS

1 lb/450 g mealy
   potatoes, diced
8 oz/225 g ground
   chicken
1 large banana
2 tbsp all-purpose flour
1 tsp lemon juice
1 onion, chopped finely
2 tbsp chopped fresh
   sage
2 tbsp butter
2 tbsp vegetable oil
⅔ cup light cream
⅔ cup chicken bouillon
salt and pepper
fresh sage leaves,
   to garnish

 easy

 serves 4

 20 minutes

 45 minutes

COOK'S TIP

Do not boil the sauce
once the cream has
been added, or it will
curdle. Cook it gently
over a very low heat.

❶ Cook the diced potatoes in a pan of boiling water for 10 minutes, or until cooked through. Drain the potatoes, and mash them until smooth. Stir in the chicken.

❷ Mash the banana and add it to the potato with the flour, lemon juice, onion, and half of the chopped sage. Season well and stir the mixture.

❸ Divide the mixture into 8 equal portions. With lightly floured hands, shape each portion into a round patty.

❹ Heat the butter and oil in a skillet, then add the potato cakes and cook for 12–15 minutes, or until cooked through, turning once. Remove from the skillet and keep warm.

❺ Stir the cream and bouillon into the skillet with the remaining chopped sage. Cook the sauce gently over a low heat for 2–3 minutes.

❻ Arrange the potato cakes on a serving plate and garnish with fresh sage leaves, then serve immediately, with the cream and sage sauce.

Chicken Risotto à la Milanese

INGREDIENTS

½ cup butter
2 lb/900 g chicken
    meat, sliced thinly
1 large onion, chopped
2½ cups risotto rice
2½ cups chicken
    bouillon
⅔ cup white wine
1 tsp crumbled saffron
salt and pepper
½ cup grated Parmesan
    cheese, to serve

❶ Heat 4 tablespoons of butter in a deep skillet and cook the chicken and onion until golden brown.

❷ Add the rice and stir well, then cook for 15 minutes.

❸ Heat the bouillon until it boils, and add it to the rice a little at a time. Add the white wine, saffron, and salt and pepper to taste, and mix well. Simmer the risotto gently for 20 minutes, stirring occasionally, and adding more bouillon if the risotto becomes too dry.

❹ Let stand for a few minutes and just before serving add a little more bouillon and simmer for an additional 10 minutes. Serve the risotto, sprinkled with the grated Parmesan cheese and the remaining butter.

 extremely easy

serves 4

10 minutes, plus 5 minutes to stand

45 minutes

COOK'S TIP
A risotto should have moist but separate grains. Bouillon should be added a little at a time and only when the last addition has been completely absorbed.

Main Meals

Chicken works well cooked with other meats and even with seafood to make hearty main-course dishes. The classic Spanish Paella is packed with exciting tastes, textures and flavors: chicken, chorizo sausage, and ham are buried with shrimp, clams, and mussels in short-grain rice flavored with saffron. Moroccan Chicken Couscous is an exotic dish of chicken with vegetables, beans, fruit, and spices, resting on a bed of couscous. Chicken with Green Olives & Pasta is an uncomplicated, tasty dish of chicken casseroled with vegetables in a wine and cream sauce.

Spanish Chicken with Garlic

INGREDIENTS

2–3 tbsp all-purpose
    flour
cayenne pepper
4 chicken joints,
    patted dry
about 4 tbsp olive oil
20 large garlic cloves,
    each halved
    and the green core
    removed
1 large bay leaf
2 cups chicken bouillon
4 tbsp dry white wine
chopped fresh parsley,
    to garnish
salt and pepper

very easy

serves 4

10 minutes

1 hour

COOK'S TIP
The cooked garlic cloves
are delicious mashed
into a purée on the side
of the plate, to be
smeared on the
chicken pieces.

❶ Put about 2 tablespoons of the flour in a plastic bag and season to taste with cayenne pepper and salt and pepper. Put a chicken piece in the bag, and shake until it is coated with the flour. Shake off the excess. Repeat with the other pieces, adding more flour and seasoning as necessary.

❷ Heat 3 tablespoons of the olive oil in a large skillet. Add the garlic cloves and fry for about 2 minutes, stirring, to flavor the oil. Remove with a slotted spoon and set aside.

❸ Add the chicken to the skillet, skin-side down, and panfry for 5 minutes, or until the skin is golden. Turn and fry for 5 minutes more, adding 1–2 tablespoons oil if necessary.

❹ Return the garlic to the pan. Add the bay leaf, bouillon, and wine, and bring to a boil, then cover the pan and simmer for 25 minutes, or until the chicken is tender and the garlic cloves are soft. Using a slotted spoon, transfer the chicken to a serving plate, and keep warm. Bring the cooking liquid to a boil with the garlic, and boil until reduced to about 1 cup plus 2 tablespoons. Season to taste.

❺ Spoon the sauce over the chicken pieces, and scatter the garlic cloves around them. Garnish with parsley and serve.

Moroccan Chicken Couscous

about 3 tbsp olive oil
8 chicken pieces, with
   bones
2 large onions, chopped
2 large garlic cloves,
   crushed
1 inch/2.5 cm piece fresh
   root ginger, peeled
   and chopped finely
5½ oz/150 g dried
   chickpeas, soaked
   overnight and drained
4 large carrots, cut into
   thick chunks
large pinch of saffron
   threads, dissolved in
   2 tbsp boiling water
grated zest of 2 lemons
2 red bell peppers, cored,
   seeded, and sliced
2 large zucchinis,
   cut into chunks
2 tomatoes, cored,
   seeded, and chopped
3½ oz/100 g dried
   apricots, chopped
½ tsp ground cumin
½ tsp ground coriander
½ tsp cayenne pepper
2½ cups water
1 tbsp butter
3⅓ cups instant couscous
salt and pepper

 very easy

 serves 4

 20 minutes,
plus 8 hours
to soak

 1 hour,
25 minutes

❶ Heat 3 tablespoons of the oil in a large flameproof casserole. Pat the chicken pieces dry with paper towels, add to the oil, skin-side down, and fry for 5 minutes, or until crisp and brown. Remove from the casserole and set aside.

❷ Add the onions to the casserole, adding a little extra oil, if necessary. Cook the onions for 5 minutes, then add the garlic and ginger, and fry for for another 2 minutes, stirring occasionally. Return the chicken pieces to the casserole. Add the chickpeas, carrots, saffron, and lemon zest. Pour in enough water to cover by 1 inch/2.5 cm, and bring to a boil.

❸ Lower the heat, cover the pan, and simmer for 45 minutes, or until the chickpeas are tender. Add the dried apricots, bell peppers, zucchinis, tomatoes, cumin, and coriander. Season to taste. Re-cover and simmer for 15 minutes more.

❹ Meanwhile, bring the water to a boil. Stir in ½ teaspoon of salt and the butter. Sprinkle in the couscous. Cover the pan tightly, remove from the heat, and let stand for 10 minutes, or until the couscous grains are tender.

❺ Fluff the couscous with a fork. Taste and adjust the seasoning of the stew. Spoon the couscous into individual bowls and serve the stew in a separate serving bowl.

Chicken Basquaise

INGREDIENTS

3 lb/1.3 kg chicken, cut
  into 8 pieces
flour, for dusting
2–3 tbsp olive oil
1 large onion, sliced
  thickly
2 bell peppers, seeded
  and cut lengthwise
  into thick strips
2 garlic cloves
5 oz/140 g spicy chorizo
  sausage, peeled,
  if necessary, and cut
  into ½ inch/1 cm
  pieces
1 tbsp tomato paste
1 cup long-grain white
  rice or medium-grain
  Spanish rice,
  such as Valencia
2 cups chicken bouillon
1 tsp crushed dried
  chilis
½ tsp dried thyme
4 oz/115 g Bayonne or
  other air-dried ham,
  diced
12 dry-cured black
  olives
2 tbsp chopped fresh
  flatleaf parsley
salt and pepper

very easy

serves 4

10 minutes

1½ hours

❶ Dry the chicken pieces with paper towels. Put about 2 tablespoons flour in a plastic bag and season with salt and pepper. Put a chicken piece in the bag, and shake it to coat the chicken. Repeat with the remaining chicken pieces.

❷ Heat 2 tablespoons of oil in a large flameproof casserole over a medium–high heat. Add the chicken and panfry for 15 minutes, or until well browned. Transfer to a plate.

❸ Heat the remaining oil in the casserole and add the onion and bell peppers. Reduce the heat to medium, and stir-fry until the vegetables begin to color and soften. Add the garlic, chorizo, and tomato paste and continue stirring for about 3 minutes. Add the rice and cook for about 2 minutes, stirring to coat, until the rice is translucent.

❹ Add the stock, crushed chilis, thyme, and salt and pepper, and stir to combine. Bring to a boil. Return the chicken to the casserole, pressing it gently into the rice. Cover the pan and cook over a very low heat for about 45 minutes, or until the chicken and rice are tender.

❺ Stir the ham, black olives, and half the parsley into the rice mixture gently. Cover the pan and heat for 5 minutes more. Sprinkle with the remaining parsley, and serve.

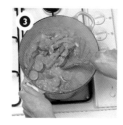

Squabs with a Fruity Rice Stuffing

INGREDIENTS

4 fresh game hens, or other free-range hens
4–6 tbsp butter, melted

STUFFING
1 cup port
1 cup raisins
1 cup dried no-soak apricots, sliced
2–3 tbsp extra-virgin olive oil
1 onion, chopped finely
1 celery stalk, sliced
2 garlic cloves, chopped
1 tsp ground cinnamon
1 tsp dried oregano
1 tsp dried mint or basil
½ tsp allspice
225 g/8 oz unsweetened chestnuts
1 cup long-grain white rice, cooked
grated zest and juice of 2 oranges
1½ cups chicken bouillon
½ cup walnut halves, toasted and chopped
2 tbsp chopped mint
2 tbsp chopped fresh flatleaf parsley
salt and pepper

❶ To make the stuffing, combine the port, raisins, and apricots in a small bowl and let stand for about 15 minutes.

❷ Heat the oil in a heavy pan, add the onion and celery, and cook for 3–4 minutes. Add the garlic, herbs, spices, and chestnuts, and cook for 4 minutes, stirring occasionally. Add the rice and pour in half the orange zest and juice and the bouillon. Simmer gently until most of the liquid is absorbed.

❸ Drain the raisins and apricots, reserving the port, and stir into the rice mixture with the walnuts, mint, and parsley, and cook for another 2 minutes. Season with salt and pepper, then remove from the heat and cool.

❹ Rub the hens inside and out with salt and pepper. Fill the cavity of each bird with stuffing, but do not pack too tightly. Tie the legs of each bird together, tucking in the tail. Form extra stuffing into balls. Arrange the birds in a roasting pan with the stuffing balls, and brush with melted butter. Drizzle any remaining butter around the pan. Pour the remaining orange zest and juice and the reserved port over the chicken.

❺ Roast in a preheated oven at 350°F/180°C for 45 minutes, basting, until cooked. Transfer to a plate, cover with foil, and let rest for 5 minutes. Serve with any pan juices.

 easy

 serves 4

20 minutes, plus 15 minutes to stand

 55 minutes, plus 5 minutes to stand

Spanish Paella

INGREDIENTS

½ cup olive oil
3 lb 5 oz/1.5 kg chicken,
    cut into 8 pieces
12 oz/350 g chorizo
    sausage, cut into
    ½ inch/1 cm pieces
4 oz/115 g cured ham,
    chopped
2 onions, chopped
2 red bell peppers,
    cored and cut into
    1 inch/2.5 cm pieces
4–6 garlic cloves
3¾ cups short-grain
    Spanish rice
2 bay leaves
1 tsp dried thyme
1 tsp saffron threads,
    crushed lightly
1 cup dry white wine
6¼ cups chicken
    bouillon
4 oz/115 g fresh peas,
    shelled, or frozen
    peas, defrosted
1 lb/450 g medium
    uncooked shrimp
8 raw jumbo shrimp,
    in shells
16 clams, scrubbed
16 mussels, scrubbed
salt and pepper
4 tbsp chopped parsley

❶ Heat half the oil in an 18 inch/46 cm paella pan or a deep, wide skillet, then add the chicken and panfry gently, turning, until golden brown. Remove from the pan and set aside.

❷ Add the chorizo and ham, and panfry for 7 minutes, stirring occasionally, until crisp. Remove and set aside.

❸ Stir the onions into the pan and cook for 3 minutes, or until soft. Add the bell peppers and garlic and cook until beginning to soften; remove and set aside.

❹ Add the remaining oil to the pan and stir in the rice to coat it. Add the bay leaves, thyme, and saffron, and stir. Pour in the wine, simmer, then pour in the bouillon, scraping the pan to stir it in. Bring to a boil, stirring often.

❺ Stir in the chorizo, ham, and chicken with the cooked vegetables, and bury them in the rice. Reduce the heat and cook for 10 minutes, stirring occasionally. Add the peas and shrimp, and cook for another 5 minutes. Push the clams and mussels into the rice. Cover, and cook gently for about 5 minutes, or until the rice is tender and the shellfish open. Discard any unopened clams or mussels. Season to taste.

❻Remove the pan from heat and let stand, covered, for about 5 minutes. Sprinkle with chopped parsley and serve.

easy

serves 4

15 minutes

1 hour

Murgh Pullau

INGREDIENTS

1¾ cups basmati rice
4 tbsp ghee or butter
1 cup slivered almonds
¾ cup unsalted, shelled pistachio nuts
4–6 boned chicken halves, skinned and each cut into 4 pieces
2 onions, sliced thinly
2 garlic cloves, chopped finely
1 inch/2.5 cm piece fresh ginger root, peeled and chopped
6 green cardamom pods, crushed lightly
4–6 whole cloves
2 bay leaves
1 tsp ground coriander
½ tsp cayenne pepper
1 cup plain yogurt
1 cup heavy cream
2–4 tbsp chopped fresh cilantro or mint
8 oz/225 g seedless green grapes, halved if large

❶ Bring a pan of salted water to a boil. Pour in the rice little by little, return to a boil, then simmer until the rice is just tender. Drain and rinse under cold running water. Set aside.

❷ Heat the ghee in a deep skillet over medium–high heat. Add the almonds and pistachios, and cook for 3 minutes, stirring, until light golden. Remove and reserve.

❸ Add the chicken to the skillet and cook for 5 minutes, or until golden, turning. Remove and reserve. Add the onions to the skillet. Cook for about 10 minutes, or until golden. Stir in the garlic, herbs, spices, and cook for 3 minutes.

❹ Add 2–3 tablespoons of the yogurt, and cook, stirring, until all the moisture evaporates. Continue adding the rest of the yogurt in the same way.

❺ Return the chicken and nuts to the skillet, and stir well to coat them with the sauce. Stir in ½ cup boiling water. Season with salt and pepper. Cover the pan and cook over a low heat for about 10 minutes, or until the chicken is cooked thoroughly. Stir in the cream, cilantro, and grapes, and remove the pan from the heat.

❻ Fork the rice into a bowl. Fold in the chicken and sauce gently. Let stand for 5 minutes, then serve.

very easy

serves 4

10 minutes,
plus 5 minutes
to stand

1 hour

Singapore Noodles

❶ To make the curry sauce, whisk the rice wine and soy into the curry powder and stir in the remaining ingredients. Stir well to combine thoroughly.

❷ Put the Chinese mushrooms in a small bowl, add enough boiling water to cover them, and soak for about 15 minutes, or until softened. Lift out the mushrooms and squeeze out the liquid. Discard any stems, then slice thinly and set aside. Soak the rice noodles according to the instructions on the package, then drain well.

❸ Heat the oil in a wok or a deep skillet over a medium heat. Add the garlic, shallots, ginger, and chiles, and stir-fry for about 30 seconds. Add the chicken and snow peas, and stir-fry for about 2 minutes. Add the Napa cabbage, shrimp, water chestnuts, mushrooms, and scallions, and stir-fry for 1–2 minutes. Add the curry sauce and noodles, and stir-fry for 5 minutes. Sprinkle with fresh cilantro, and serve.

 extremely easy

 serves 4

 30 minutes,
  plus 15 minutes
  to soak

 12 minutes

SINGAPORE CURRY SAUCE

2 tbsp rice wine, or dry sherry
2 tbsp soy sauce
3 tbsp medium or hot Madras
  curry powder
1 tbsp sugar

$1^{2}/_{3}$ cups canned
  coconut milk
1 tsp salt
black pepper,
  to taste

Simmered Stew of Meat, Chicken, Vegetables & Fruit

INGREDIENTS

2 lb/900 g boneless pork, or pork pieces
2 bay leaves
1 onion, chopped
8 garlic cloves, chopped finely
2 tbsp chopped fresh cilantro
1 carrot, sliced thinly
2 celery stalks, diced
2 chicken bouillon cubes
½ chicken, in portions
4–5 ripe tomatoes, diced
½ tsp mild chili powder
grated zest of ¼ orange
¼ tsp ground cumin
juice of 3 oranges
1 zucchini, cut into bite-size pieces
¼ cabbage, sliced thinly and blanched
1 apple, cut into bite-size pieces
about 10 prunes, pitted
¼ tsp ground cinnamon
pinch of dried ginger
2 hard chorizo sausages, about 12 oz/350 g in total, diced
salt and pepper

 extremely easy

 serves 4

 20 minutes

 2 hours, 20 minutes

❶ Put the pork, bay leaves, onion, garlic, cilantro, carrot, and celery in a large pan, and fill it to the top with cold water. Bring to a boil, skim off the scum that has formed on the surface, then reduce the heat and simmer the meat and vegetables gently for 1 hour.

❷ Add the bouillon cubes to the pan, along with the chicken, tomatoes, chili powder, orange zest, and cumin. Continue to cook for an additional 45 minutes, or until the chicken is tender. Spoon off the fat that forms on the top of the liquid.

❸ Add the orange juice, zucchini, cabbage, apple, prunes, cinnamon, ginger, and chorizo. Continue to simmer for an additional 20 minutes, or until the zucchini is tender and the chorizo is cooked through.

❹ Season with salt and pepper, and serve at once.

Chicken Halves in Green Salsa with Sour Cream

INGREDIENTS

4 chicken halves, boned
flour, for dredging
2–3 tbsp butter, or
   butter and oil
1 lb/450 g mild green
   salsa, or
   puréed tomatillos
1 cup chicken bouillon
1–2 garlic cloves,
   chopped finely
3–5 tbsp chopped fresh
   cilantro
½ green chile, seeded
   and chopped
½ tsp ground cumin
salt and pepper

TO SERVE

1 cup sour cream
several leaves Romaine
   lettuce, shredded
3–5 scallions, sliced
   thinly
roughly chopped fresh
   cilantro

❶ Sprinkle the chicken with salt and pepper, then dredge in flour. Shake off the excess.

❷ Melt the butter in a skillet, then add the chicken halves and cook over a medium–high heat, turning once, until they are golden but not cooked through—they continue to cook slightly in the sauce. Remove from the skillet and set aside.

❸ Place the salsa, chicken bouillon, garlic, cilantro, chile, and cumin in a pan, and bring to a boil. Reduce the heat to a low simmer. Add the chicken halves to the sauce, and spoon the sauce over the chicken. Continue to cook until the chicken is cooked through.

❹ Remove the chicken from the pan and season with salt and pepper. Serve with the sour cream, shredded lettuce, scallions, and cilantro leaves.

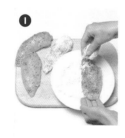

 extremely easy

 serves 4

 15 minutes

 30 minutes

Chicken with Purslane & Red Chili

INGREDIENTS

juice of 1 lime
6 garlic cloves, chopped
finely
¼ tsp dried oregano
¼ tsp dried marjoram
¼ tsp dried thyme
½ tsp ground cumin
1 chicken, cut into
4 pieces
about 10 large mild
chilis, such as pasilla,
dried
2 cups boiling water
2 cups chicken bouillon
3 tbsp extra-virgin
olive oil
1 lb 9 oz/700 g
tomatoes, charred
under the broiler,
skinned, and seeded
handful of corn tortilla
chips, crushed
several large handfuls
of purslane, cut into
bite-size lengths
½ lime
salt and pepper
lime wedges, to serve

❶ Combine the lime juice, half the garlic, the oregano, marjoram, thyme, cumin, and salt to taste. Rub the mixture over the chicken and let marinate for at least 1 hour, or overnight in the refrigerator.

❷ Place the chilis in a pan, and pour the boiling water over them. Cover the pan and let stand for 30 minutes. Remove the stems and seeds, and purée the flesh in a food processor or a blender, adding enough bouillon to make a smooth paste. Add the remaining bouillon, mix well, and set aside.

❸ Heat 1 tablespoon of oil in a skillet. Add the chili paste with the tomatoes and remaining garlic. Panfry over a medium heat, stirring, until reduced by half. Set aside.

❹ Remove the chicken from the marinade, reserving any juices. Brown the chicken pieces in the remaining oil, then place in a flameproof casserole. Add any reserved juices and the reduced chili sauce. Cover, and simmer over a low heat for about 30 minutes, or until the chicken is tender.

❺ Stir the crushed tortillas into the sauce, and cook for a few minutes. Add the purslane. Season the casserole with salt, pepper, and a squeeze of lime, and serve garnished with lime wedges.

 very easy

 serves 4

 15 minutes, plus 1 hour to marinate and to stand

 45 minutes

 ❷

 ❹

Jambalaya

INGREDIENTS

2 tbsp vegetable oil
2 onions, chopped
    roughly
1 green bell pepper,
    seeded and chopped
    roughly
2 celery stalks, chopped
    roughly
3 garlic cloves, chopped
    finely
2 tsp paprika
10½ oz/300 g skinless,
    boneless chicken
    halves, chopped
3½ oz/100 g boudin
    sausages, chopped
3 tomatoes, skinned
    and chopped
2 cups long-grain rice
3¾ cups hot chicken or
    fish bouillon
1 tsp dried oregano
2 fresh bay leaves
12 large jumbo shrimp
    tails
4 scallions, chopped
    finely
2 tbsp chopped fresh
    parsley
salt and pepper
salad, to serve

❶ Heat the vegetable oil in a large skillet and add the onions, bell pepper, celery, and garlic. Panfry for 8–10 minutes, or until all the vegetables have softened. Add the paprika and fry for another 30 seconds. Add the chicken and sausages and cook for 8–10 minutes, or until lightly browned. Add the tomatoes and cook for 2–3 minutes, or until they have collapsed.

❷ Add the rice to the pan and stir well. Pour in the hot bouillon, oregano, and bay leaves, and stir well. Cover and simmer for 10 minutes over a very low heat.

❸ Add the shrimp and stir well. Cover again and cook for an additional 6–8 minutes, or until the rice is tender and the shrimp are cooked through.

❹ Stir in the scallions and parsley, then season to taste. Serve immediately, accompanied by a salad.

 extremely easy

 serves 4

 15 minutes

 45 minutes

Chicken & Mango Stir-Fry

INGREDIENTS

6 boneless, skinless
   chicken thighs
1 inch/2.5 cm piece
   fresh ginger, grated
1 garlic clove, crushed
1 small red chile, seeded
1 large red bell pepper
4 scallions
1½ cups snow peas
1 cup baby corn
1 large firm, ripe mango
2 tbsp sunflower oil
1 tbsp light soy sauce
3 tbsp rice wine or
   sherry
1 tsp sesame oil
salt and pepper

❶ Cut the chicken into long, thin strips and place in a bowl. Mix together the ginger, garlic, and chile, then stir the mixture into the chicken strips to coat them evenly.

❷ Slice the bell pepper thinly, cutting at a diagonal angle. Trim the scallions and slice them at a diagonal angle. Cut the snow peas and corn in half at a diagonal angle. Peel the mango, remove the pit, and slice it thinly.

❸ Heat the oil in a wok or a large skillet over a high heat. Add the chicken and stir-fry for 4–5 minutes, or until it just turns golden brown. Add the bell peppers and stir-fry over a medium heat for 4–5 minutes to soften them. Add the scallions, corn, and snow peas, and stir-fry for a minute more.

❹ Mix together the soy sauce, rice wine or sherry, and sesame oil, and stir into the wok. Add the mango and stir gently for 1 minute to heat thoroughly. Adjust the seasoning with salt and pepper to taste, and serve immediately.

extremely easy

serves 4

15 minutes

15 minutes

Green Chicken Curry

INGREDIENTS

6 boneless, skinless
  chicken thighs
1¾ cups coconut milk
2 garlic cloves, crushed
2 tbsp Thai fish sauce
2 tbsp green curry paste
12 baby eggplants
3 green chiles, chopped
  finely
3 kaffir lime leaves,
  shredded
4 tbsp chopped fresh
  cilantro
boiled rice, to serve

❶ Cut the chicken into small, even-sized cubes. Pour the coconut milk into a wok or a large skillet over a high heat, and bring to a boil.

❷ Add the chicken, garlic, and fish sauce to the skillet, and bring back to a boil. Lower the heat and simmer gently for 30 minutes, or until the chicken is tender.

❸ Remove the chicken from the mixture with a slotted spoon, set aside and keep warm.

❹ Stir the green curry paste into the skillet, then add the eggplants, chiles, and lime leaves, and simmer the curry for 5 minutes.

❺ Return the chicken to the skillet and bring to a boil. Adjust the seasoning to taste with salt and pepper, then stir in the cilantro. Serve the curry with plain rice.

 extremely easy

 serves 4

 5 minutes

 55 minutes

COOK'S TIP

Baby eggplants, also called "Thai apple" or "Thai pea" eggplants, are traditionally used in this curry. If you cannot find them in an Asian food shop, Japanese eggplant would be a good substitute, chopped small.

Braised Chicken with Garlic & Spices

4 garlic cloves, chopped
4 shallots, chopped
2 small red chiles,
    seeded and chopped
1 lemon grass stalk,
    chopped finely
1 tbsp chopped fresh
    cilantro
1 tsp shrimp paste
½ tsp ground cinnamon
1 tbsp tamarind paste
2 tbsp vegetable oil
8 small chicken
    drumsticks or thighs
1¼ cups chicken
    bouillon
1 tbsp Thai fish sauce
1 tbsp smooth peanut
    butter
salt and pepper
4 tbsp chopped toasted
    peanuts

❶ Place the garlic, shallots, chiles, lemon grass, cilantro, and shrimp paste in a mortar, and grind them with a pestle to an almost smooth paste. Add the cinnamon and tamarind paste.

❷ Heat the oil in a wok or a wide skillet. Add the chicken drumsticks and fry them, turning often, until they are golden brown on all sides. Remove them from the wok and keep hot. Pour off any excess fat.

❸ Add the spice paste to the wok or skillet, and stir over a medium heat until lightly browned. Stir in the bouillon, and return the chicken to the wok.

❹ Bring the mixture to a boil, then cover the pan tightly, lower the heat, and simmer for 25–30 minutes, stirring occasionally, until the chicken is tender and cooked thoroughly. Stir in the fish sauce and peanut butter, and simmer gently for another 10 minutes.

❺ Adjust the seasoning with salt and pepper to taste, and scatter the toasted peanuts over the chicken. Serve the dish hot, with colorful stir-fry vegetables and noodles.

 very easy

 serves 4

 10 minutes

 35 minutes

Whole-Wheat Spaghetti with Suprêmes of Chicken Nell Gwyn

INGREDIENTS

⅛ cup canola oil
3 tbsp olive oil
4 x 8 oz/225 g chicken
   suprêmes
⅔ cup orange brandy
2 tbsp all-purpose flour
⅔ cup freshly squeezed
   orange juice
1 oz/25 g zucchini, cut
   into short, thin sticks
1 oz/25 g red bell
   pepper, cut into
   short, thin sticks
1 oz/25 g leek, finely
   shredded
14 oz/400 g dried
   whole-wheat
   spaghetti
3 large oranges, peeled
   and cut into
   segments
zest of 1 orange, cut into
   very fine strips
2 tbsp chopped fresh
   tarragon
⅔ cup ricotta cheese
salt and pepper
fresh tarragon leaves,
   to garnish

❶ Heat the canola oil and 1 tablespoon of the olive oil in a skillet. Add the chicken and cook quickly until golden brown. Add the orange brandy and cook for 3 minutes. Sprinkle the flour over the mixture and cook for 2 minutes.

❷ Lower the heat and add the orange juice, zucchini, bell pepper, and leek, and season. Simmer for 5 minutes, or until the sauce has thickened.

❸ Meanwhile, bring a pan of salted water to a boil. Add the spaghetti and 1 tablespoon of the olive oil, and cook for 10 minutes. Drain, then transfer to a serving dish and drizzle the remaining oil over the pasta.

❹ Add half the orange segments, half the orange zest, the tarragon, and ricotta cheese to the sauce in the skillet, and cook for 3 minutes.

❺ Place the chicken on top of the pasta and pour a little sauce over the top, then garnish with orange segments, zest, and tarragon leaves. Serve immediately.

 very easy

 serves 4

 15 minutes

 30 minutes

Chicken & Wild Mushroom Lasagna

INGREDIENTS

butter, for greasing
14 sheets pre-cooked
    lasagna
3¾ cups béchamel
    Sauce
¾ cup grated
    Parmesan cheese

CHICKEN & WILD
MUSHROOM SAUCE
2 tbsp olive oil
2 garlic cloves, crushed
1 large onion, chopped
    finely
8 oz/225 g wild
    mushrooms, sliced
2½ cups ground chicken
3 oz/85 g chicken livers,
    chopped finely
4 oz/115 g prosciutto,
    diced
⅔ cup Marsala wine
10 oz/280 g canned
    chopped tomatoes
1 tbsp chopped fresh
    basil leaves
2 tbsp tomato paste
salt and pepper

❶ Begin by making the chicken and wild mushroom sauce. Heat the olive oil in a large pan, add the garlic, onion, and mushrooms, and fry, stirring frequently, for 6 minutes.

❷ Add the ground chicken, chicken livers, and prosciutto, and continue frying over a low heat for 12 minutes, or until the meat has browned.

❸ Stir the Marsala wine, tomatoes, basil, and tomato paste into the mixture in the pan, and cook for 4 minutes. Season to taste with salt and pepper, then cover the pan, and simmer for 30 minutes. Uncover the pan, stir the mixture, and simmer for another 15 minutes.

❹ Grease an ovenproof dish lightly with butter. Arrange sheets of lasagna over the base of the dish. spoon a layer of chicken and wild mushroom sauce over them, then spoon a layer of béchamel sauce over the top. Place another layer of lasagna on top, and repeat the layering twice, finishing with a layer of béchamel sauce. Sprinkle the grated cheese over the top layer, and bake the lasagna in a preheated oven at 375°F/190°C for 35 minutes, or until golden brown and bubbling. Serve immediately.

easy

serves 4

20 minutes

1¾ hours

Chicken with Green Olives & Pasta

INGREDIENTS

3 tbsp olive oil
2 tbsp butter
4 chicken halves, part-
  boned
1 large onion, chopped
  finely
2 garlic cloves, crushed
2 red, yellow, or green
  bell peppers, cored,
  seeded, and cut into
  large pieces
9 oz/250 g white
  mushrooms, sliced
  or cut into four
6 oz/175 g tomatoes,
  skinned and halved
⅔ cup dry white wine
1½ cups pitted green
  olives
4–6 tbsp heavy cream
14 oz/400 g dried pasta
salt and pepper
chopped flatleaf parsley,
  to garnish

❶ Heat 2 tablespoons of the oil and the butter in a skillet. Add the chicken halves, and panfry until they are golden brown all over. Remove the chicken from the skillet.

❷ Add the onion and garlic to the skillet, and fry over a medium heat until they begin to soften. Add the bell peppers and mushrooms, and fry for 2–3 minutes. Add the tomatoes and season to taste. Transfer the vegetables to a casserole dish, and arrange the chicken on top of them.

❸ Add the wine to the pan and bring to a boil. Pour the wine over the chicken. Cover the pan and cook in a preheated oven at 350°F/180°C for 50 minutes.

❹ Add the olives to the casserole and mix them in. Pour in the cream, cover, and return to the oven for 10–20 minutes.

❺ Meanwhile, bring a large pan of lightly salted water to a boil. Add the pasta and the remaining oil, and cook until the pasta is tender but still firm to the bite. Drain the pasta well and transfer it to a serving dish.

❻ Arrange the chicken on top of the pasta, spoon the sauce over the top, garnish with the parsley, and serve immediately. Alternatively, place the pasta in a large serving bowl and serve it separately from the vegetables.

very easy

serves 4

10 minutes

1½ hours

Creamy Chicken & Potato Casserole

INGREDIENTS

2 tbsp vegetable oil
¼ cup butter
4 chicken portions,
    about 8 oz/225 g each
2 leeks, sliced
1 garlic clove, crushed
4 tbsp all-purpose flour
3¾ cups chicken
    bouillon
1¼ cups dry white wine
4½ oz/125 g baby
    carrots, halved
    lengthwise
4½ oz/125 g baby corn,
    halved lengthwise
1 lb/450 g small new
    potatoes
1 bouquet garni
⅔ cup heavy cream
salt and pepper

❶ Heat the oil in a large skillet. Cook the chicken for 10 minutes, turning until browned all over. Transfer the chicken to a casserole dish using a perforated spoon.

❷ Add the leek and garlic to the skillet and cook for 2–3 minutes, stirring. Stir in the flour and cook for another minute. Remove the skillet from the heat and stir in the bouillon and wine. Season well.

❸ Return the pan to the heat and bring the mixture slowly to a boil. Stir in the carrots, corn, potatoes, and add the bouquet garni.

❹ Transfer the mixture to the casserole dish. Cover the dish and cook in a preheated oven, 350°F/180°C, for 1 hour.

❺ Remove the casserole from the oven and stir in the cream. Return to the oven, uncovered, and cook for another 15 minutes. Remove the bouquet garni and discard it. Taste the sauce and adjust the seasoning, if necessary. Serve the casserole with plain rice and broccoli or other vegetables.

very easy

serves 4

10 minutes

1 hour,
40 minutes

Potato Crisp Pie

INGREDIENTS

2 large waxy potatoes,
  sliced
¼ cup butter
1 skinned and boned
  chicken half, about
  6 oz/175 g
2 garlic cloves, crushed
4 scallions, sliced
¼ cup all-purpose flour
⅔ cup dry white wine
⅔ cup heavy cream
8 oz/225 g broccoli
  florets
4 large tomatoes, sliced
3 oz/85 g Gruyère
  cheese, sliced
1 cup plain yogurt
⅔ cup rolled oats,
  toasted

easy

serves 4

15 minutes

45 minutes

VARIATIONS

Add chopped nuts,
such as pine nuts,
to the topping, for
extra crunch.

❶ Cook the potatoes in a pan of boiling water for 10 minutes. Drain and set aside.

❷ Meanwhile, melt the butter in a skillet. Cut the chicken into strips and cook for 5 minutes, turning. Add the garlic and scallions, and cook for another 2 minutes.

❸ Stir in the flour and cook for 1 minute. Add the wine and cream, little by little. Bring to a boil, stirring, then reduce the heat until the sauce simmers, and cook for 5 minutes.

❹ Meanwhile, blanch the broccoli in boiling water, then drain and refresh in cold water.

❺ Place half of the potatoes in the base of a pie dish, and top with half of the tomatoes and half of the broccoli.

❻ Spoon the chicken sauce on top and repeat the layers in the same order once more.

❼ Arrange the Gruyère cheese on top and spoon the yogurt over the top. Sprinkle with the oats and cook in a preheated oven, 400°F/200°C, for 25 minutes, or until the top has turned golden brown. Serve the pie immediately.

Chicken with Creamy Zucchini & Lime Stuffing

INGREDIENTS

1 chicken, weighing
5 lb/2.25 kg
oil for brushing
9 oz/250 g zucchini
2 tbsp butter
juice of 1 lime

STUFFING
3 oz/85 g zucchini
¾ cup medium-fat
soft cheese
finely grated zest of
1 lime
2 tbsp fresh bread
crumbs
salt and pepper

easy

serves 4

15 minutes

1 hour, 50
minutes

❶ To make the stuffing, trim the zucchini and grate roughly, then mix with the cheese, lime zest, bread crumbs, and salt and pepper.

❷ Ease the skin of the chicken breast away from the meat.

❸ Push the stuffing under the skin with your fingers, to cover the chicken meat evenly.

❹ Place the chicken in a baking pan, then brush with oil and roast it in a preheated oven, 375°F/190°C, for 20 minutes per 1 lb 2 oz/500 g, plus 20 minutes, or until the juices run clear when the thickest part of the chicken is pierced with a skewer.

❺ Meanwhile, trim the remaining zucchini and cut it into long, thin strips with a potato peeler or a sharp knife. Sauté the strips in the butter and lime juice until they are just tender. Place the cooked chicken on a serving plate and scatter the sauteed zucchini around it. Serve hot.

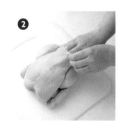

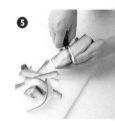